Christmas

Templates to Tangle

Delightful Design Templates for Tangling, Doodling, and Coloring

ISBN-10: 1-5091-0141-1
ISBN-13: 978-1-5091-0141-2

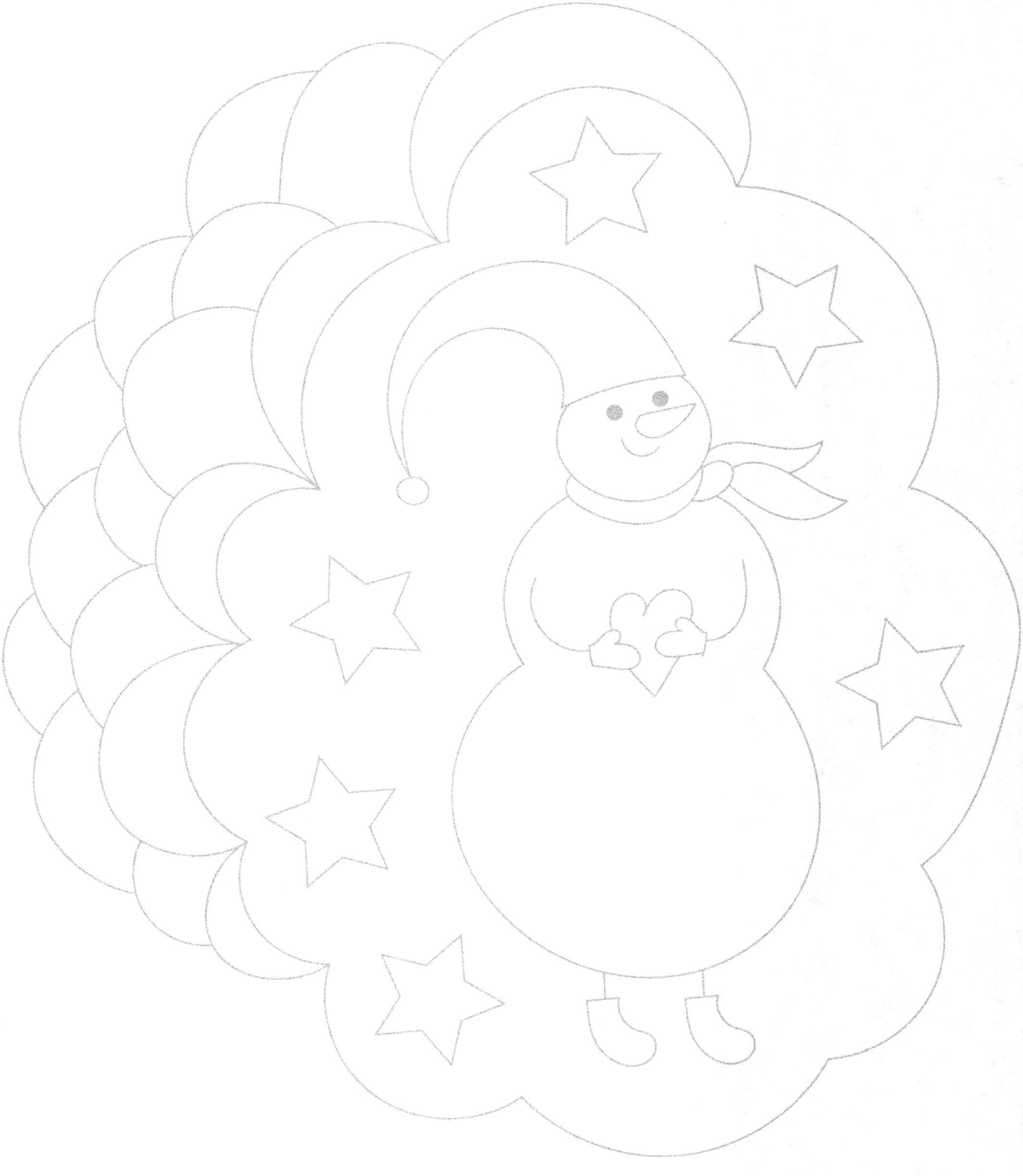

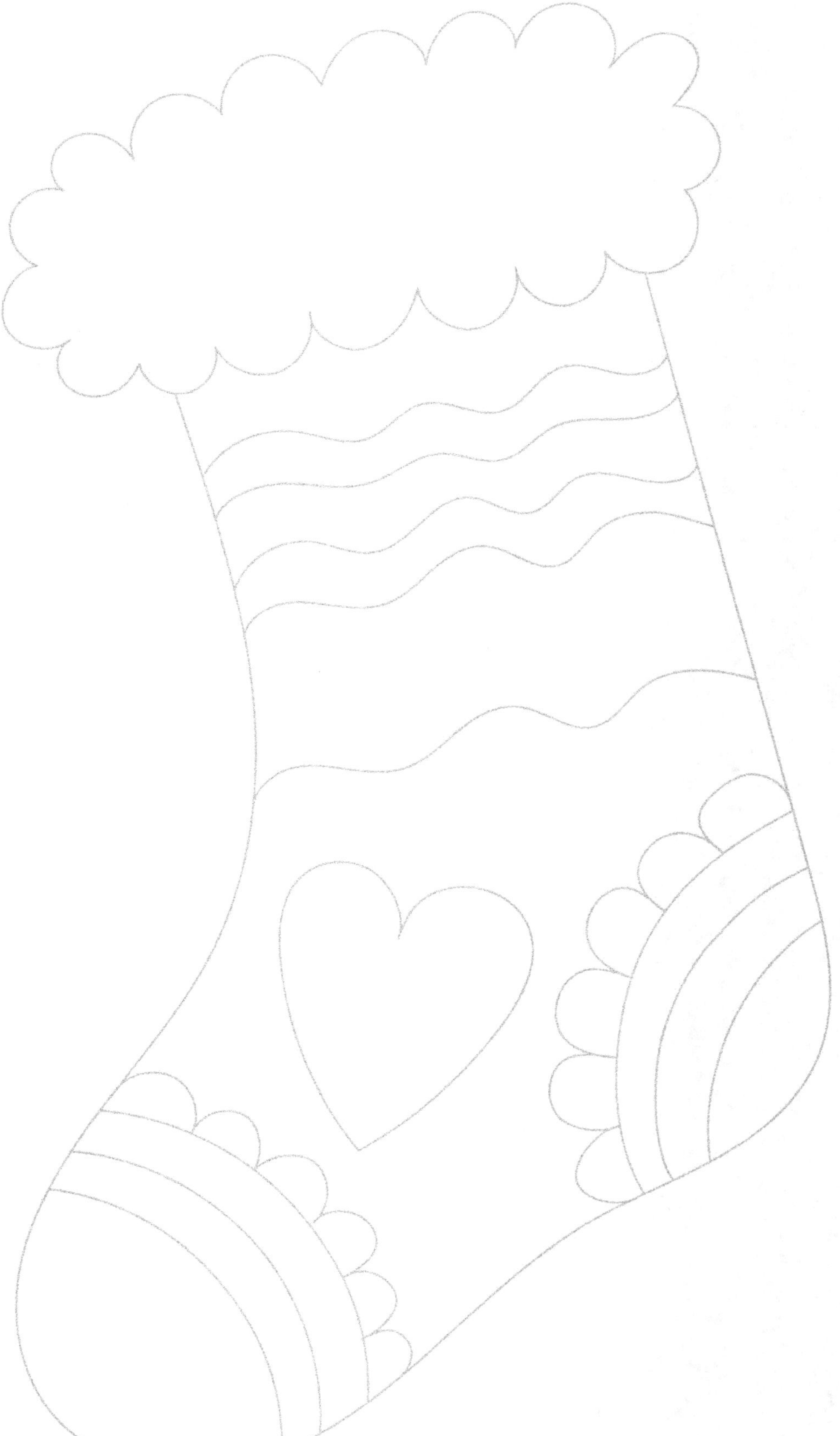

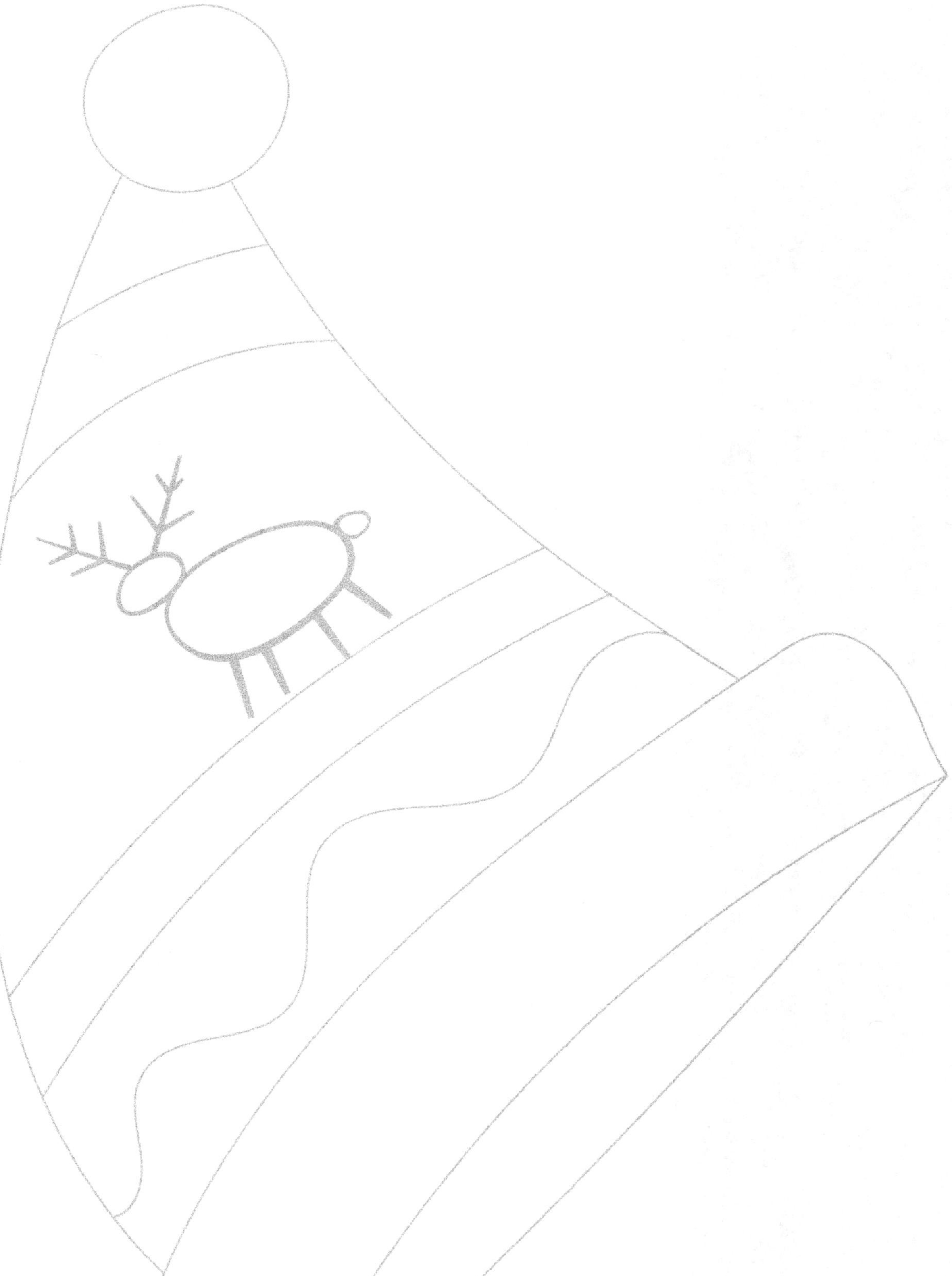

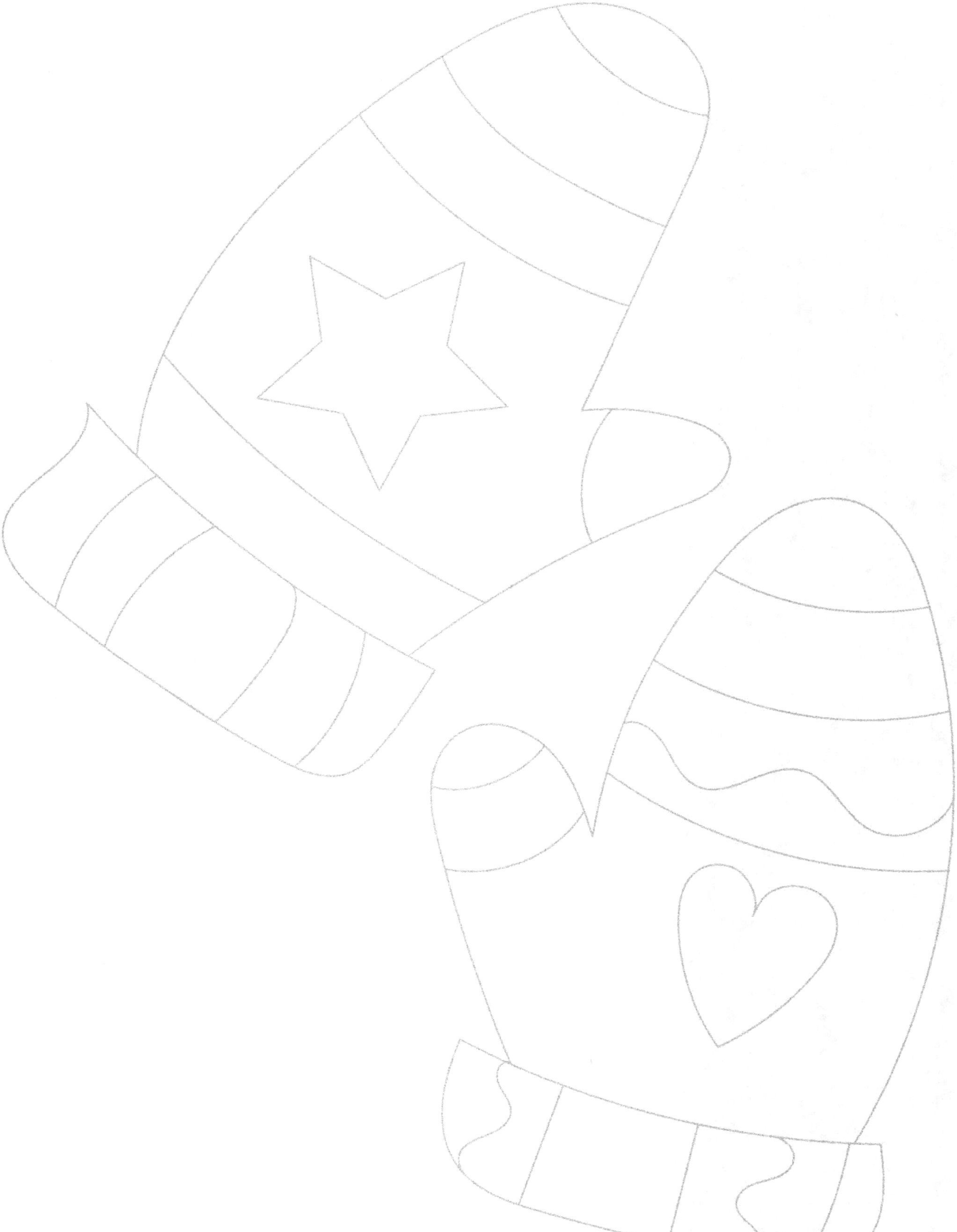

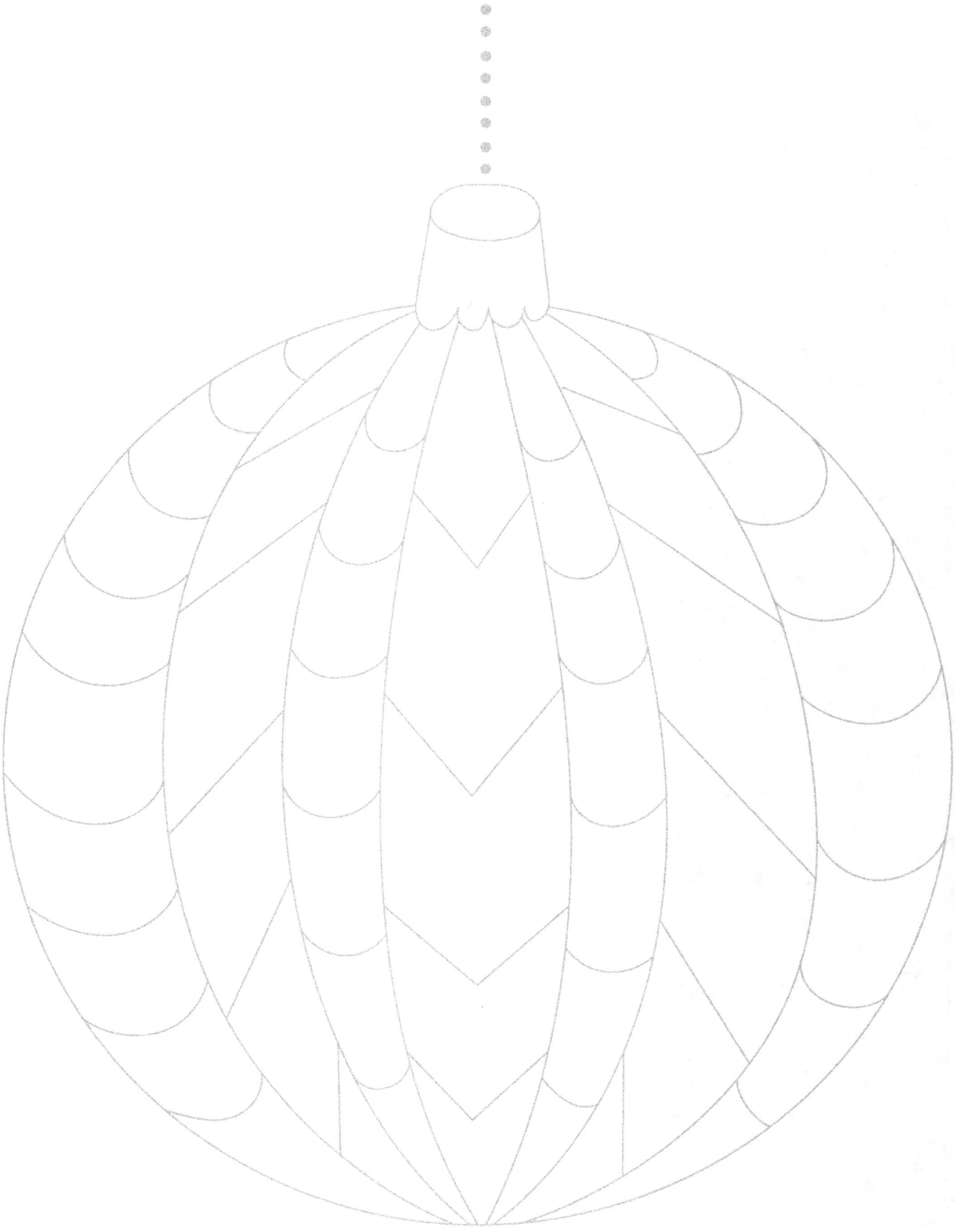

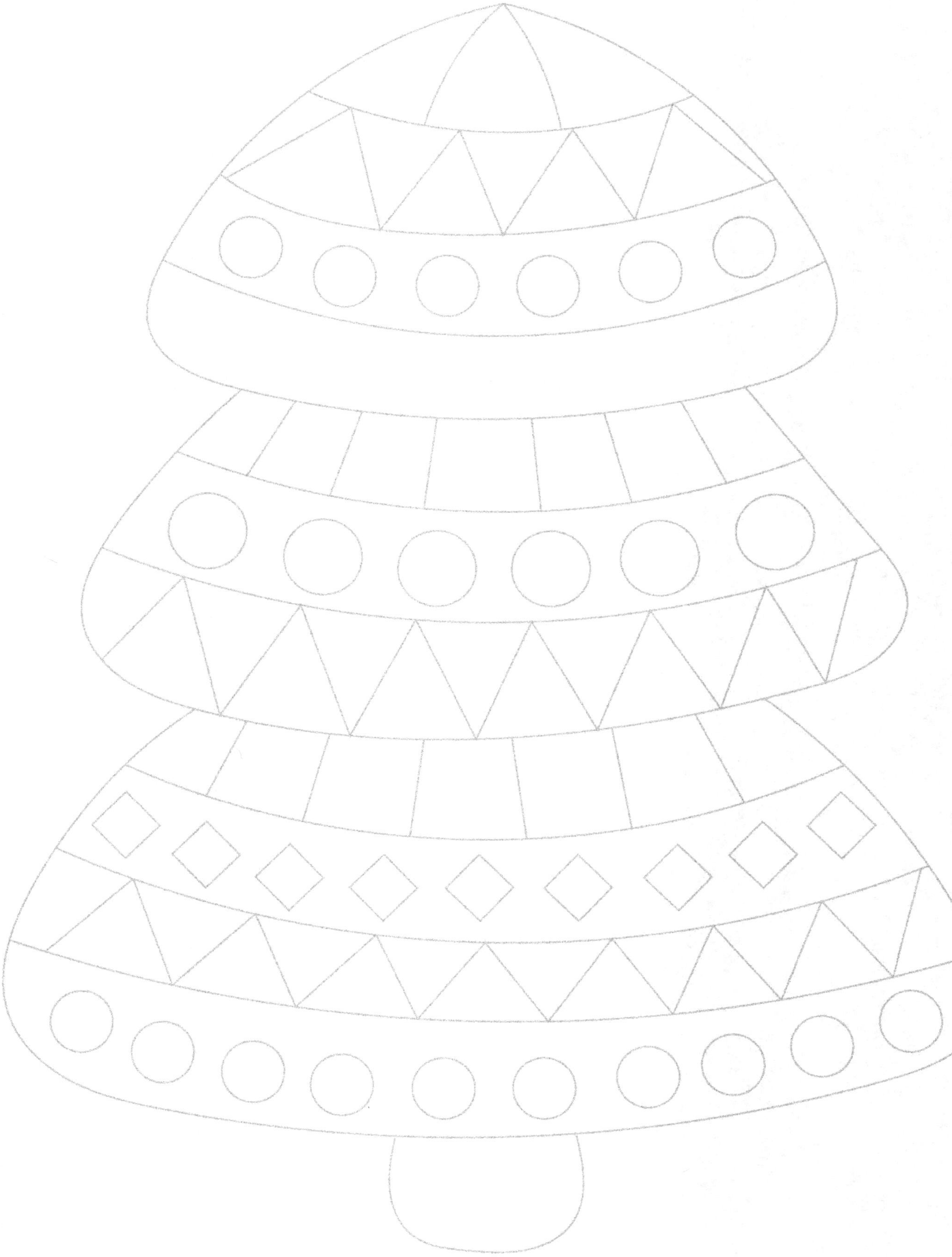

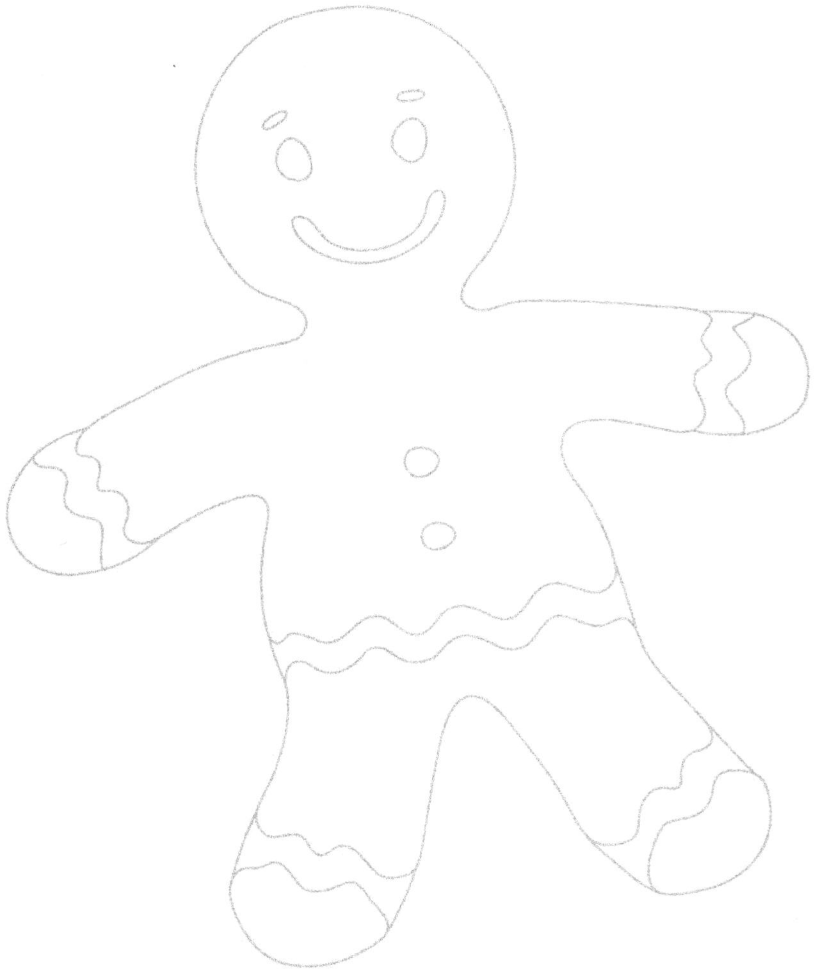
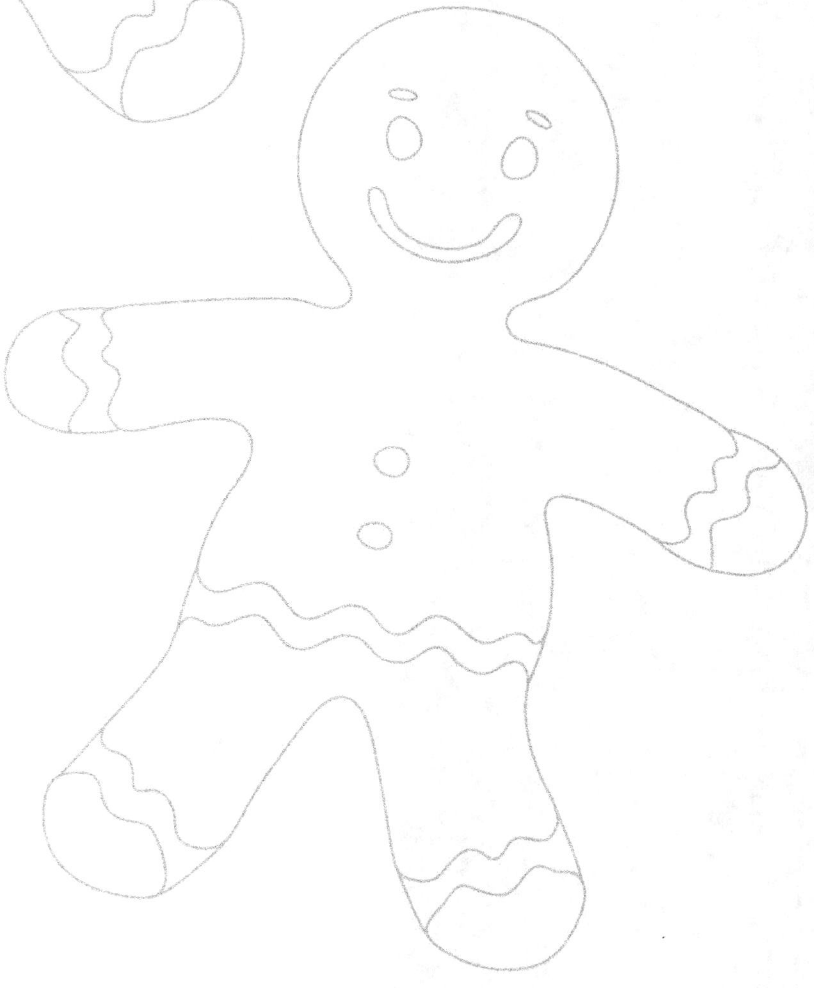

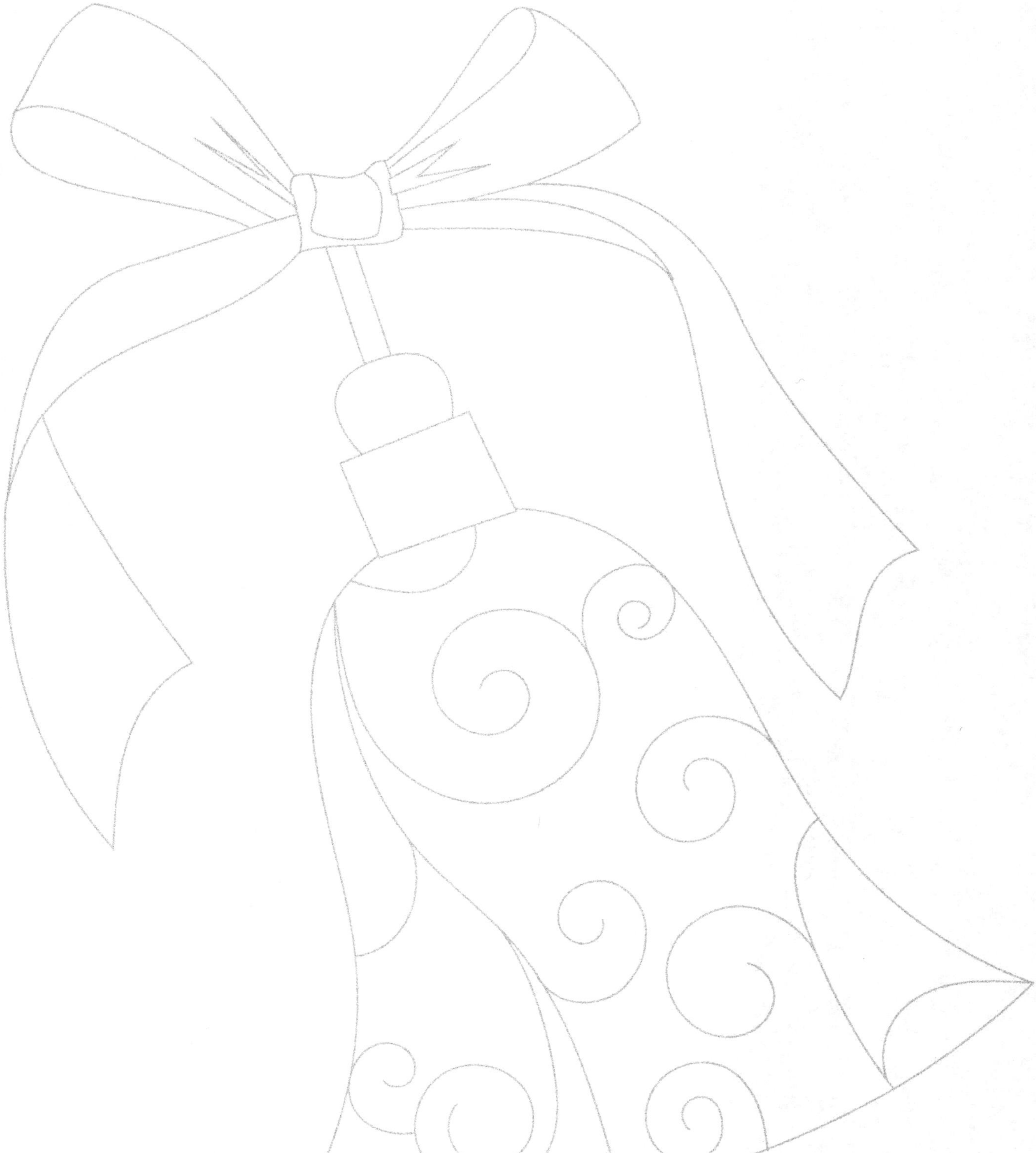

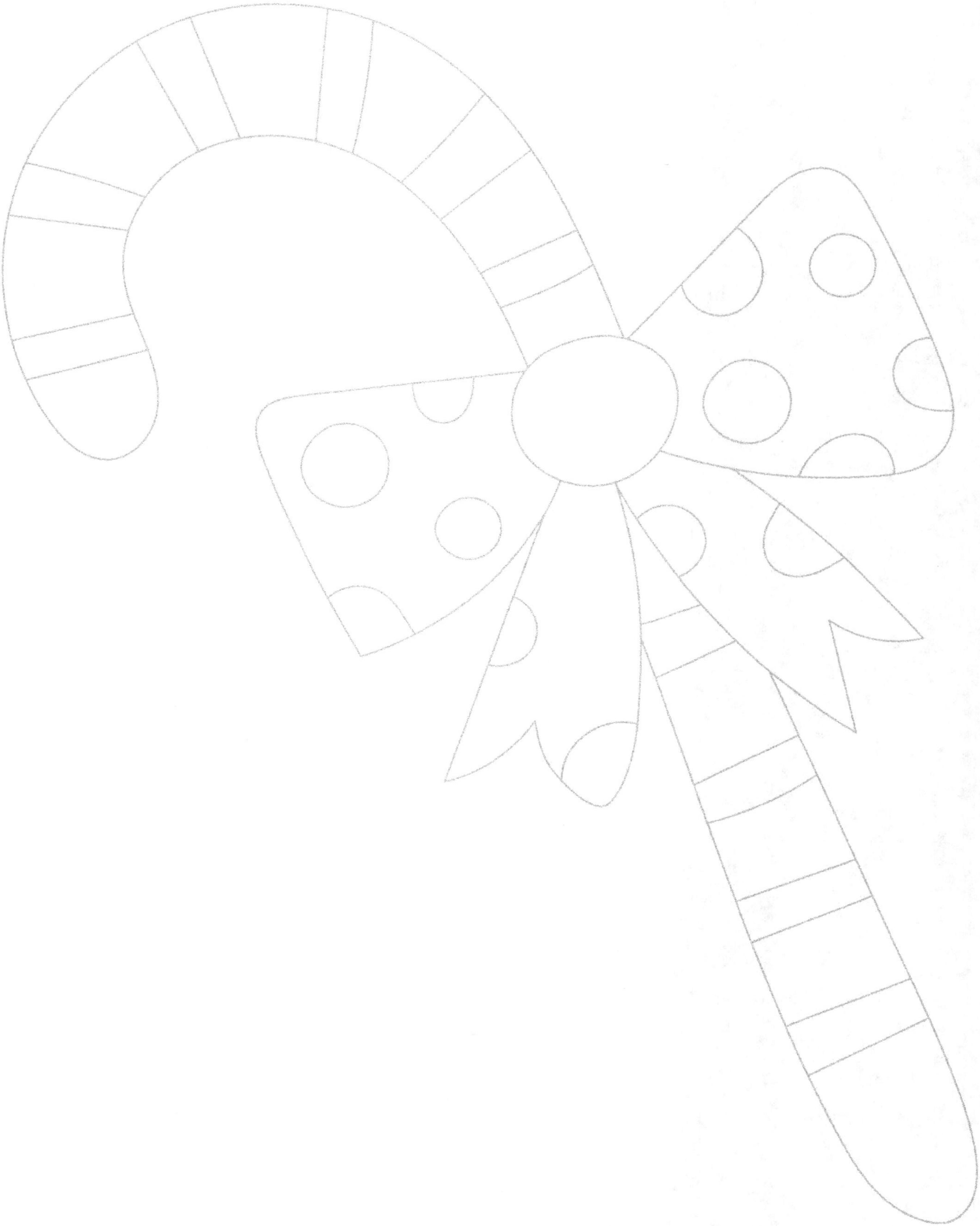

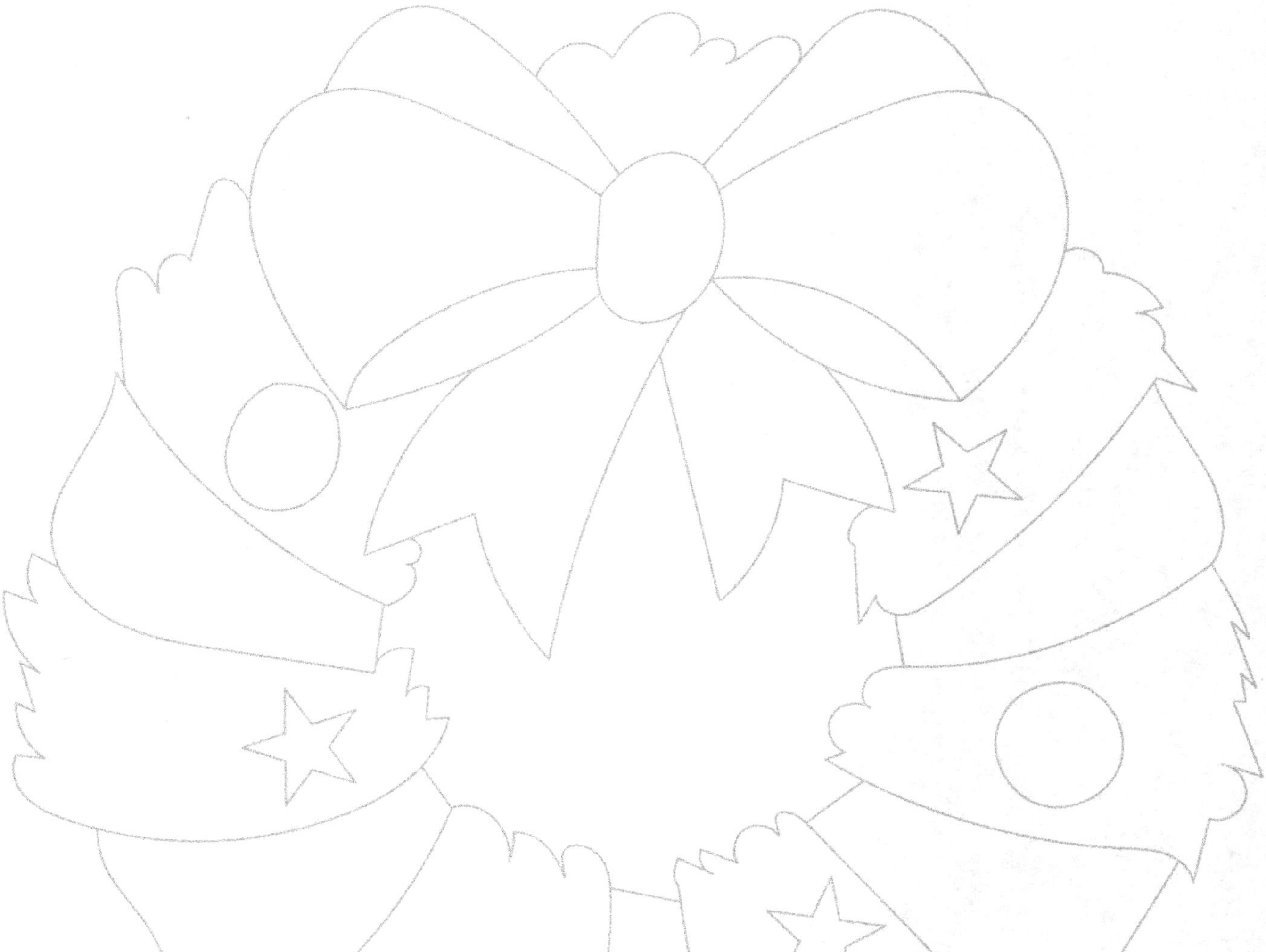

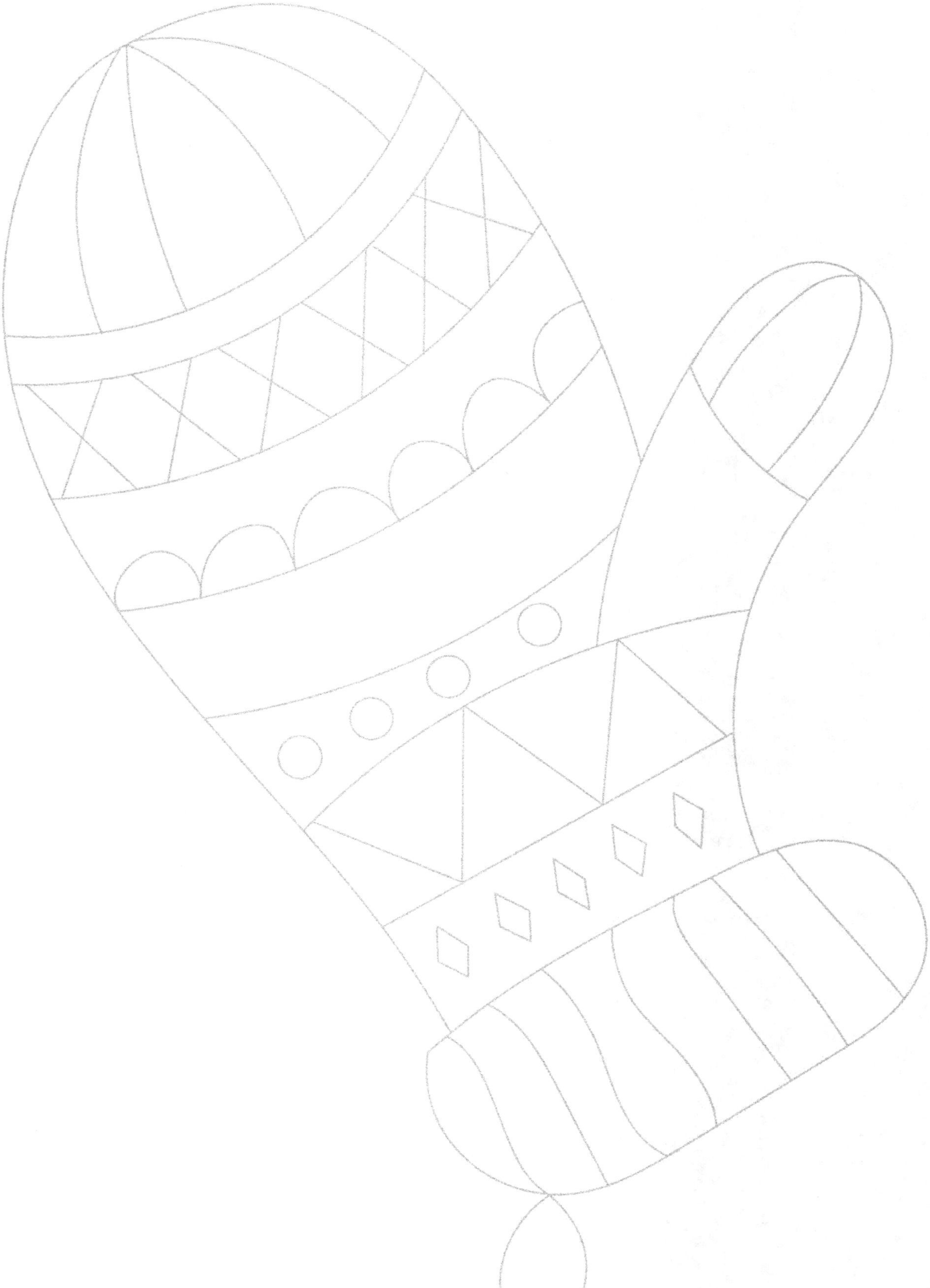

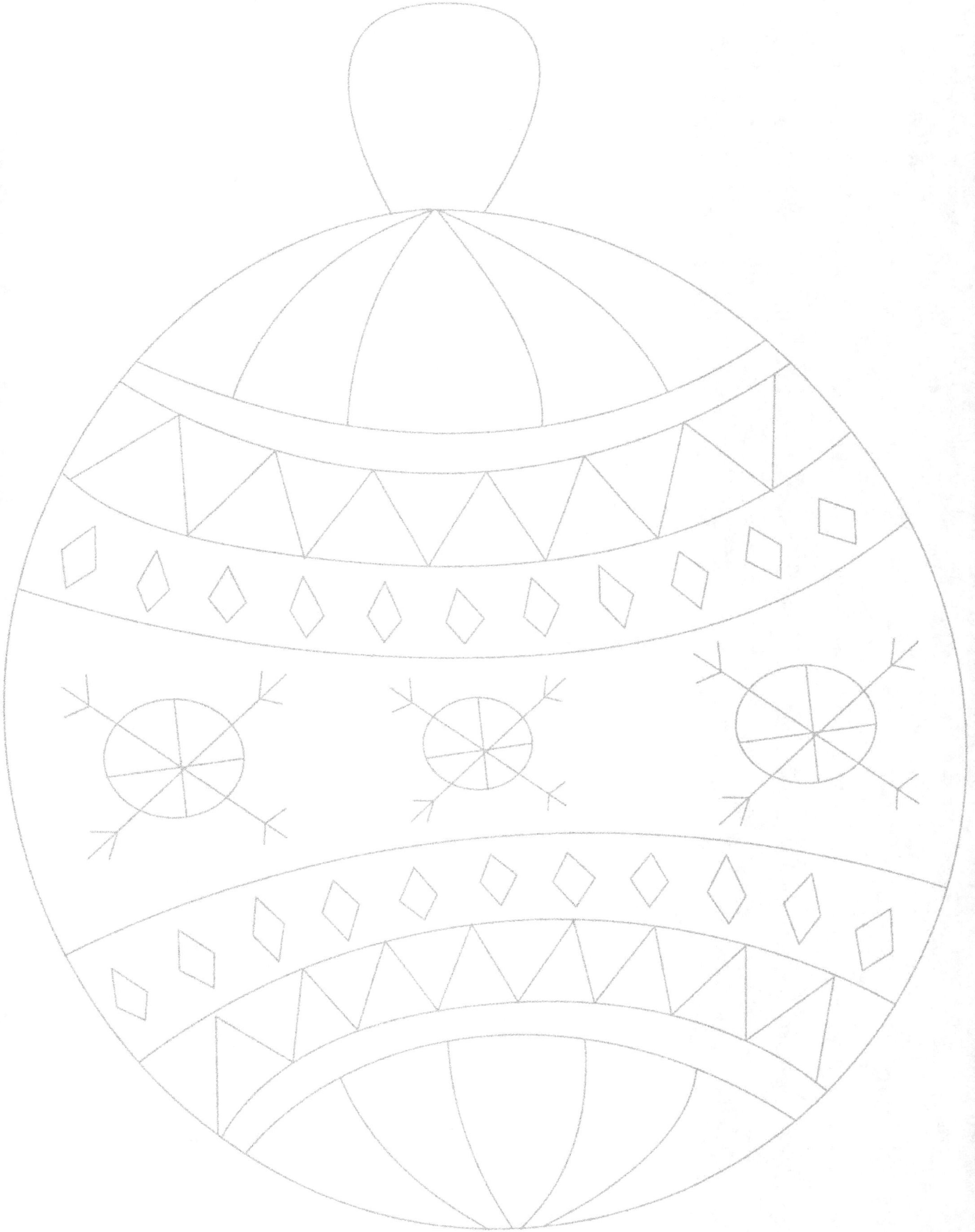

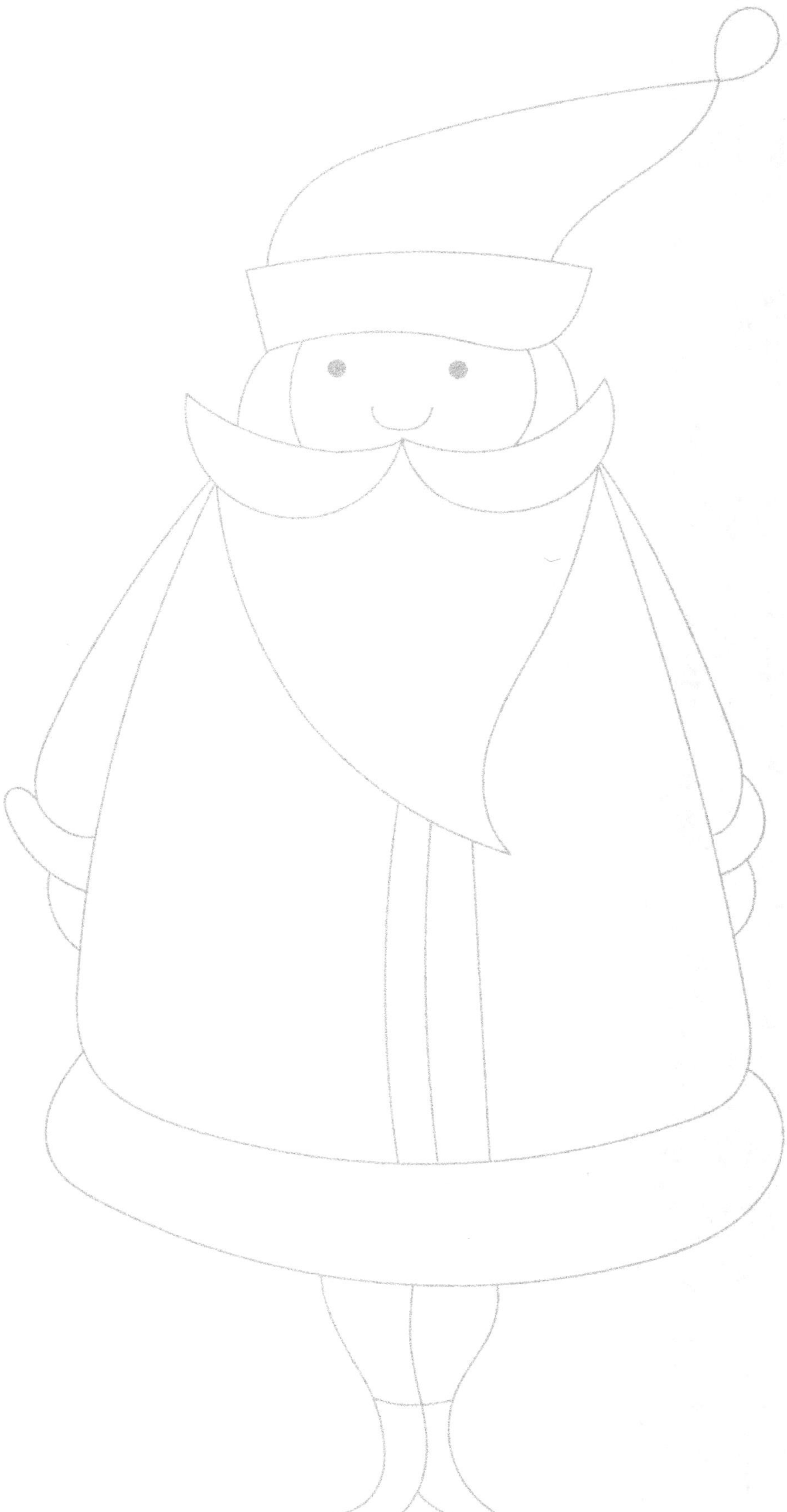

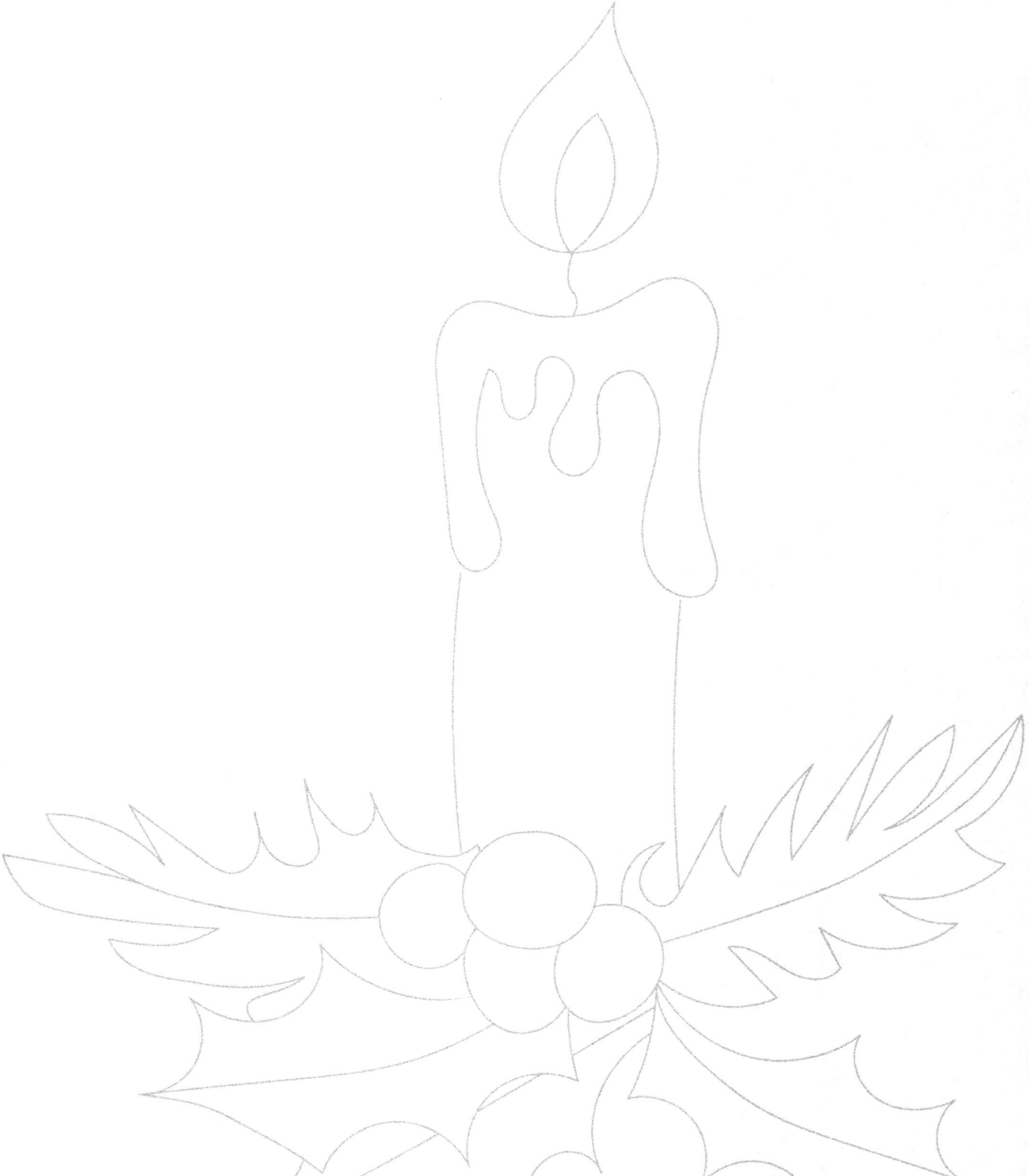

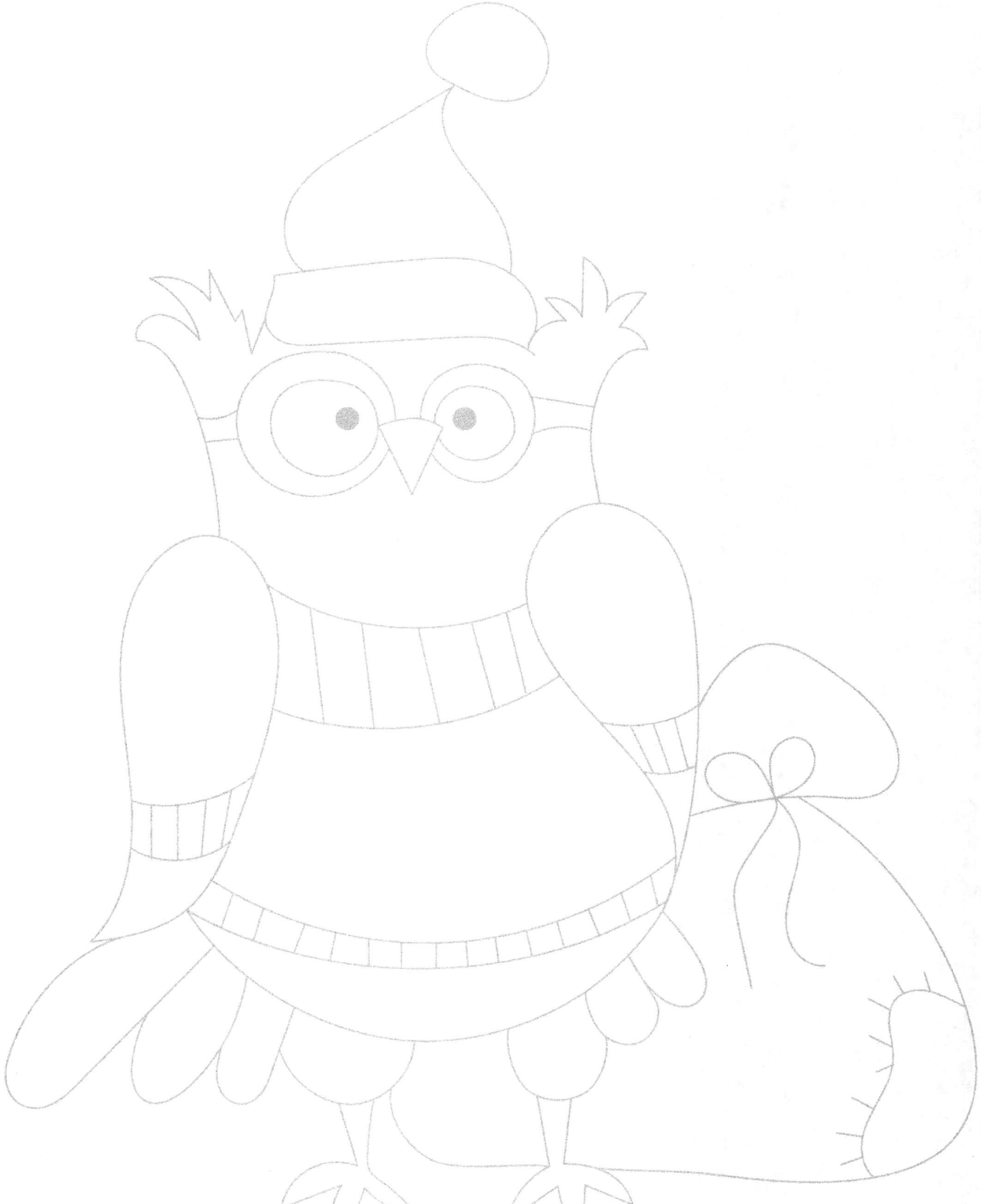

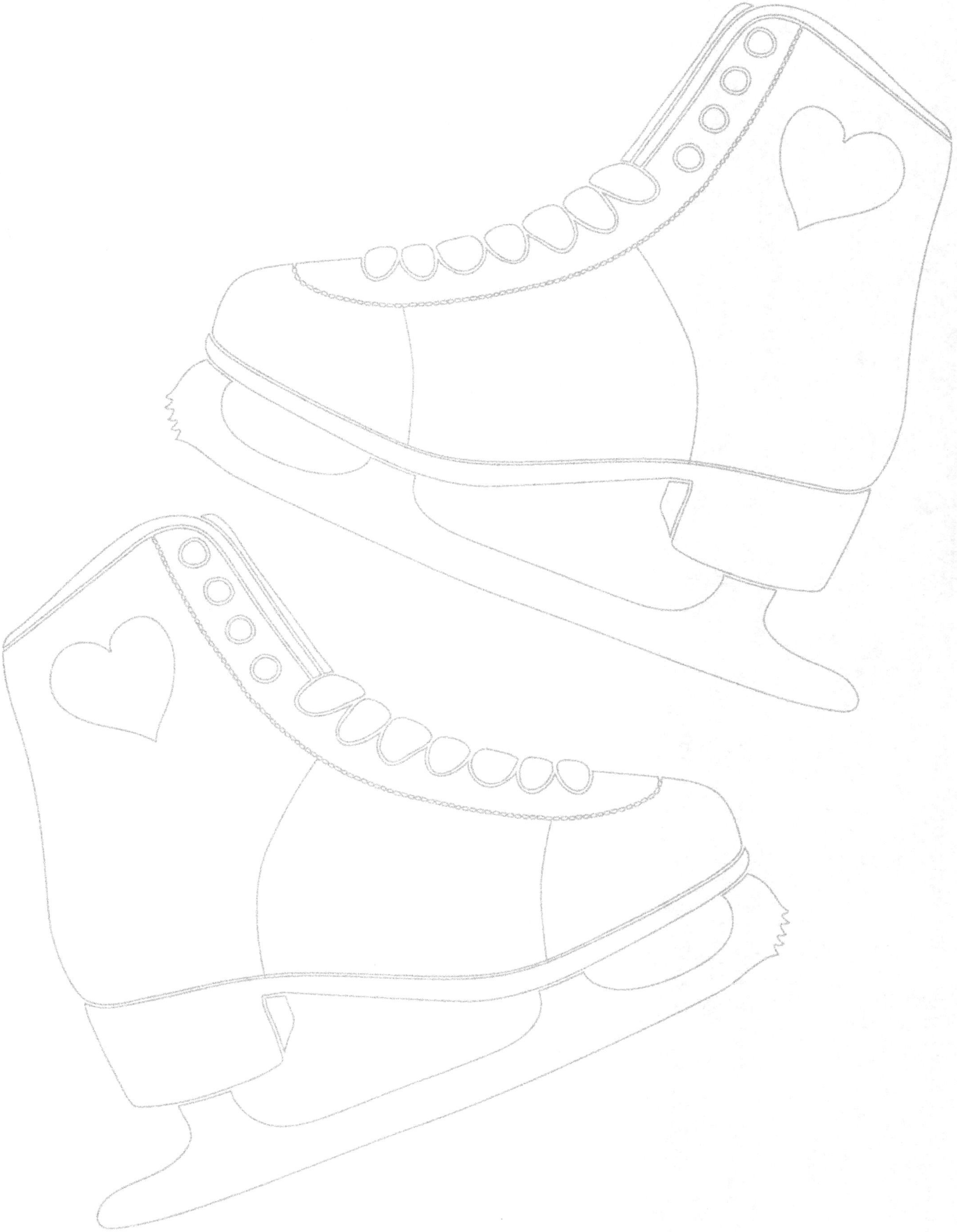

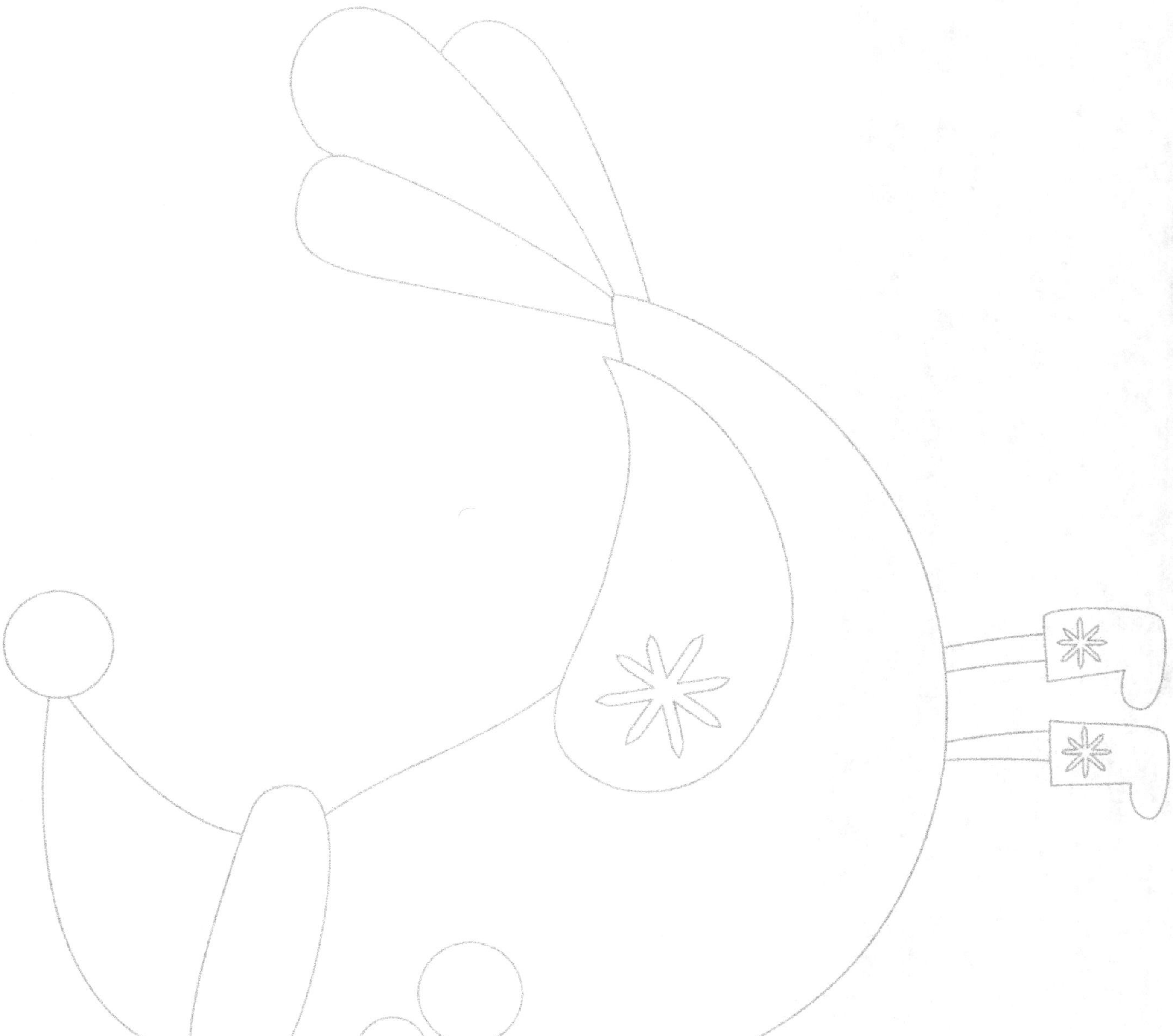

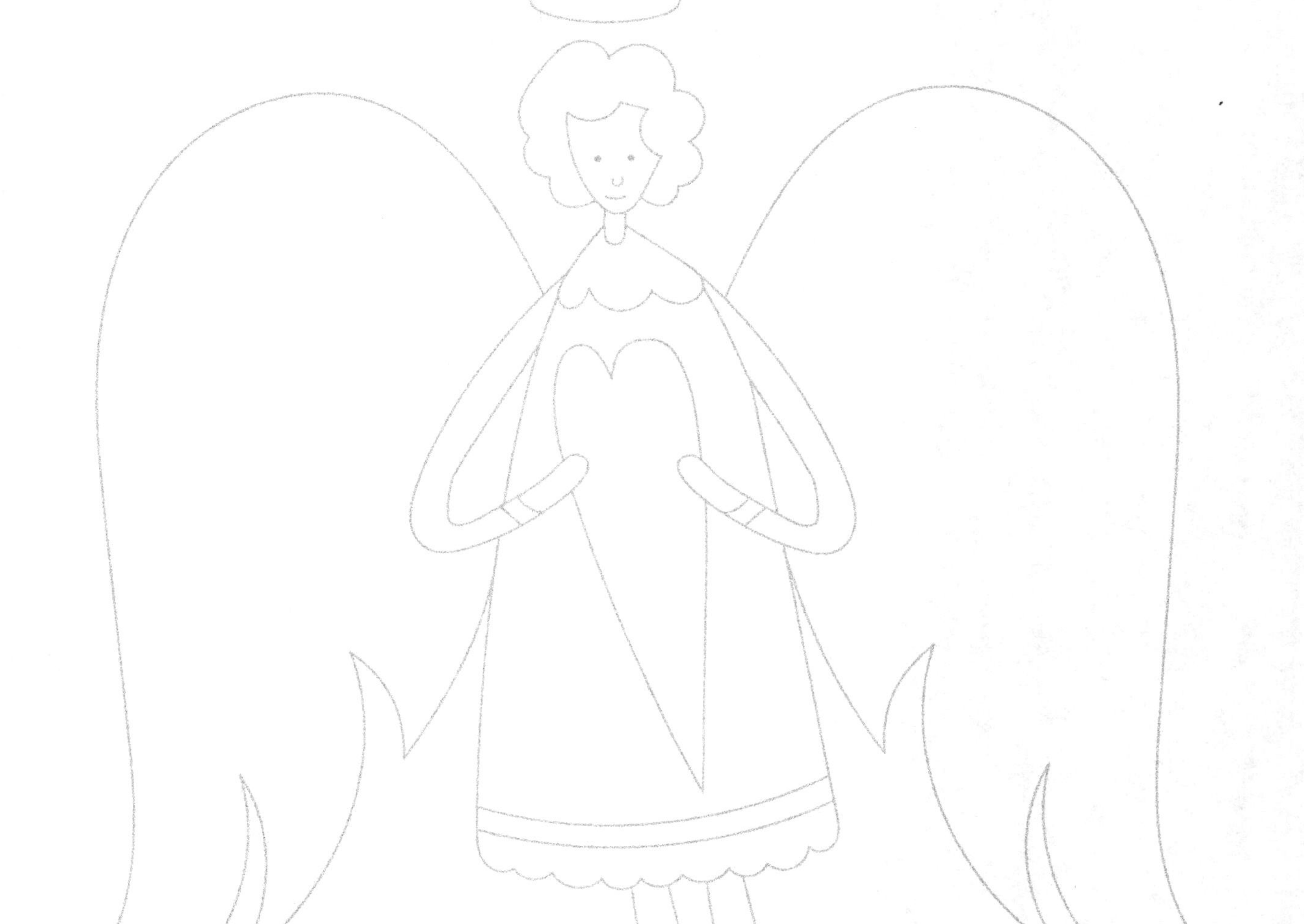

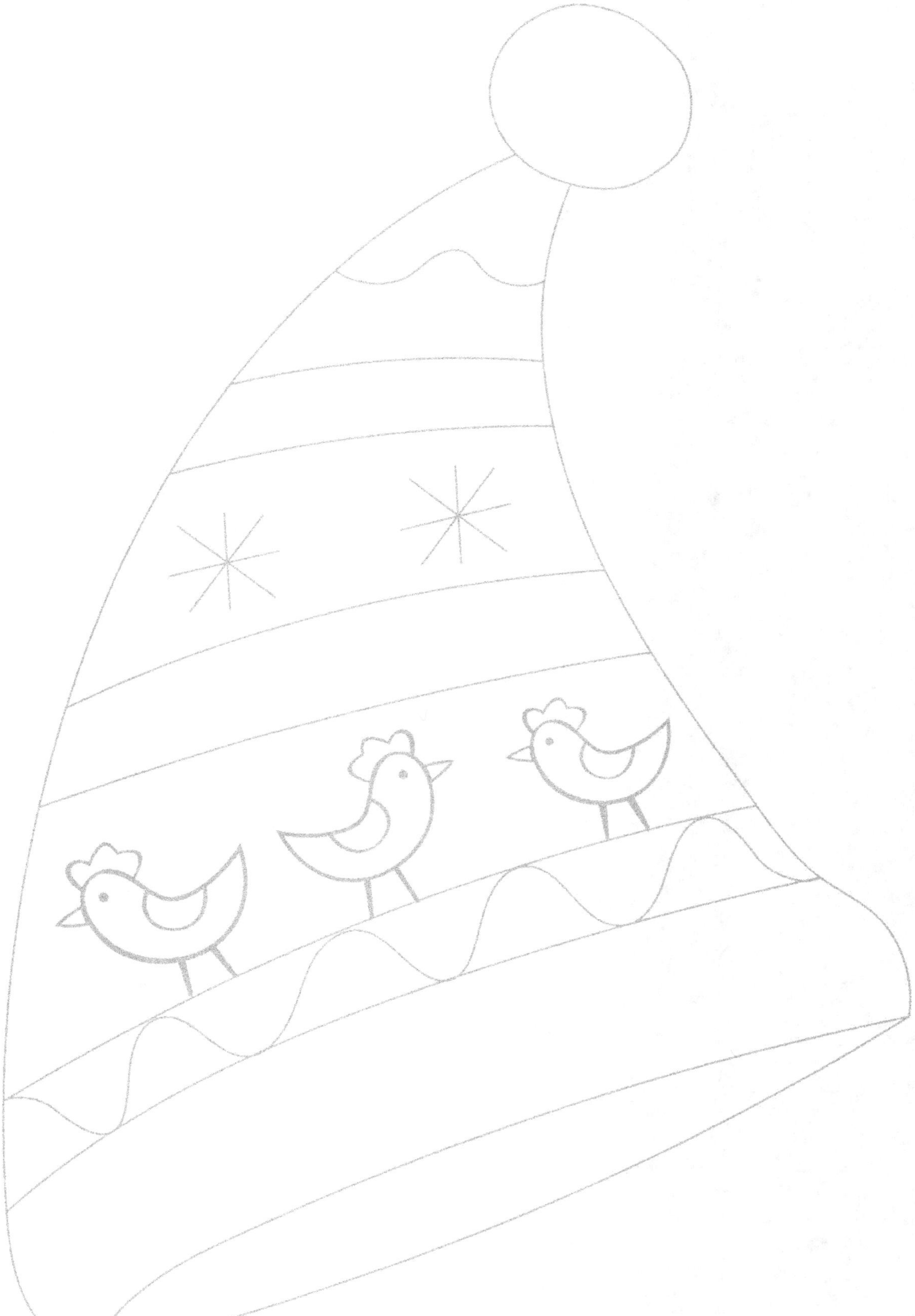

www.ingramcontent.com/pod-product-compliance
Lightning Source LLC
Chambersburg PA
CBHW080652180526
45168CB00008B/3393
9781509101412